SEXUAL ABUSE

A RAPHA RECOVERY BOOK

SEXUAL ABUSE

CYNTHIA A. KUBETIN
&
JAMES D. MALLORY, JR., M.D.

RAPHA PUBLISHING/WORD INC.
HOUSTON AND DALLAS, TX

SEXUAL ABUSE
By Cynthia A. Kubetin &
James D. Mallory, Jr., M.D.
Copyright © 1992 by Rapha Publishing/
Word, Inc., Houston and Dallas, TX

First printing 1992
ISBN: 0–945276–39–7
Printed in the United States of America

CONTENTS

CONTENTS

THE DARKNESS— A DEFINITION

What are the boundaries of sexual abuse? Who can be its victims, and what does it include?

Anyone can be a victim of sexual abuse, and any sexual activity carried out in an inappropriate context is abusive. Sexual abuse can be defined broadly as "any sexual activity, verbal, visual or physical, engaged in without consent, which may be emotionally or physically harmful and which exploits a person in order to meet another person's sexual or emotional needs. The person does not consent or refuse because of age, circumstances, level of understanding and dependency or relationship to the offender."*

* Robert S. McGee and Dr. Harry Schaumburg, *Renew: Hope for Victims of Sexual Abuse* (Houston: Rapha Publishing, 1990), p. 5.

Verbal sexual abuse consists of remarks including sexual threats, innuendoes, comments about a person's body, solicitation, harassment, coarse jesting, inappropriate sexual talking and sexual name–calling—any verbal expression with intent to arouse or stimulate.

Visual sexual abuse includes voyeurism, exhibitionism, viewing of pornographic material, of genitals, or of any sexual activity such as masturbation or intercourse.

Physical sexual abuse includes any inappropriate form of touching, from hugging to rape. Rubbing, holding, and kissing for the purpose of sexual gratification are examples. Also included in physical sexual abuse are oral, genital, anal, and breast stimulation, and penetration by penis, fingers, or any other body part or object, of mouth, anus, or vagina.

Ritualistic sexual abuse, a topic of overriding importance, is discussed in the following chapter.

Every victim, whether having experienced a one–time incident or multiple incidents, and whether over a long or short period of time, needs to recover from the effects of the abuse. God truly wants to heal victims so that nothing from the past will keep them from being whole persons in Christ.

Some victims are confused about whether they have been abused or not. Perhaps the only memory from so long ago is so vague that its reality is in doubt. Memory blocks, however, are often a symptom of abuse having occurred.

Psalms 51:6, a scripture that asks God for renewal of the innermost parts and for wisdom, is recommended as a daily prayer. It should provide help in remembering only that which is necessary for recovery, and allowing God to bring about insights and memories according to His timing so they can be dealt with one by one.

The following lists include common difficulties experienced by victims of sexual abuse. Not everyone who has these symptoms is a victim of sexual abuse, but readers who are wrestling with several of these symptoms may want to consider asking God for guidance into restoration. The key to recovery is to seek His help regarding the truth and allow Him to guide you out of darkness.

Some possible effects of sexual abuse in children (toddlers, preschoolers, school–age children, teenagers) include:

- Nightmares
- Pseudo–maturity
- Low self–esteem
- Outbursts of anger
- Withdrawal
- Violent play
- Fear of undressing
- Fear of being alone

Some possible effects of sexual abuse in female victims are:

- Secrecy
- Nightmares
- Insomnia
- Seductive behavior
- Depression
- Promiscuity
- Memory blocks
- Eating disorders

The effects of sexual abuse in male victims may surface as:

- Self–hate
- Suicidal feelings
- Confusion of identity
- Stomachaches
- Depression
- Feelings of betrayal
- Nervousness
- Withdrawal

These are but a few of the possible effects sexual abuse can produce in children, women, and men. For an expanded list of these, you can consult *Beyond the Darkness*, by Cynthia Kubetin and James Mallory, Jr., M.D. (Rapha Publishing/Word, Inc., 1992).

In Utter Darkness— The Horror of Ritualistic Abuse

—By James D. Mallory, Jr., M.D.

Ritualistic sex abuse (not so isolated or so rare as once believed) represents the ultimate in human degradation, torture, mind control, and destructiveness.

The majority of such abusers are involved in satanic rituals and worship. Abusers can include the child's own parents, neighbors, baby–sitters, special friends, or others to whom the child's care has been entrusted, in day–care centers, schools, pre–school, church, or camps.

The components of ritualistic abuse fall into four areas: physical, sexual, psychological, and spiritual. *Physical* abuse includes essentially every form of torture ever described, including beatings, cuttings, tattooing, painful electrical shock to genitals, puncture wounds, injections, being hung in various positions; withholding water, food, and sleep; nearly drowning; being buried alive; and being forced to consume blood, feces, urine, or body parts. It may include multiple sexual attacks from members of the group, insertion of painful instruments in body orifices, forced sexual activity with animals, infants, or the dead.

Psychological abuse, which is designed to gain total control over the person, is carried out by physical threats, with some of the mentioned tortures actually being carried out. Victims may be forced to engage in repulsive and often illegal activities and then told this has sealed their fate so they can never play any role in society again except as a cult member. They are brainwashed against family (if family members are not members of the cult), church, and society in general, resulting in making victims believe the only place they can exist is in the cult itself. Various mind–controlling techniques are utilized, such as food–, water–, and sleep–deprivation; long indoctrination sessions; use of drugs, threats, and torture; and programming for specific destructive activities.

Spiritual abuse consists of forcing victims to participate in rituals, activities, and instructions that induce the belief they are totally separated from God and totally controlled by Satan. They are often told they have spirit demons that will control them and punish them if they fail to obey. These people may, in fact, be under demonic influence. The younger individuals are when ritual abuse begins, the greater the emotional damage and the likelihood of their being indoctrinated and incorporated into the cult's beliefs and actions.

Signs and symptoms that should raise suspicion of ritual abuse include special fears, dreams, preoccupations, behaviors, descriptions of peculiar events, and physical symptoms. Special fears include such themes as death, devils, demons, monsters, ghosts, being confined, being harmed, being kidnapped, something bad happening to family or them, or the presence of something bad or scary inside the person's body. Dreams or nightmares may include the same themes.

Preoccupations include body excrement and body functioning, genitals, and the general fears mentioned above. Behaviors are sadistic and sexual toward others, animals, and toys. Victims may engage in strange songs or chants or in making various signs or marks that are reflective of the cult's rituals.

Children may describe unusual events at school, church, camp, or wherever the abuse is occurring. Suspicion should be aroused when children talk about special pills, drugs, candy, or shots they are getting. They may describe people in strange costumes doing strange or sexual things. Costumes may include those of benign TV characters or scary or devilish characters. Descriptions of photographs, nudity, or strange play with animals or adults should be taken very seriously.

Physical signs may be bleeding from the vagina or rectum or infection in these areas. Unexplained or strange pains, bruises, or markings on the body may be found. Such children are also very prone to a whole host of physiological symptoms such as headache, stomachache, bowel dysfunction, and sleep disturbance. Because of the extreme stress on the nervous system, virtually any so–called psychosomatic symptom—skin rashes, seizure-like episodes, dizziness, anesthesia in various parts of the body—may occur.

Without professional help, the outcome for these victims is very grim. Many become so brainwashed and indoctrinated that they remain in the cult as abusers themselves. Those who get away from the perpetrators and try to live a normal life are plagued with a host of physical, emotional, spiritual, and behavioral problems. These people are often treated for psychosomatic illnesses, hysteria and other personality disorders, depression, phobias, panic attacks, obsessions, and schizophrenia.

If the underlying trauma from the ritual abuse is not treated, victims will never experience adequate healing. Unfortunately, the underlying trauma may not even be remembered. The very mental mechanism that helps people survive this kind of trauma also can block conscious recall years later. This phenomenon, called *dissociation*, may come into play in persons who have been overwhelmed with severe abuse, torture, or terror, particularly during childhood.

The general process of healing of the survivor of ritual sex abuse is much the same as for other abuses, but requires a therapist cognizant of the additional precautions and needs of its trauma and aftermath.

Also, becoming part of a new, powerful, loving, supportive group can promote further healing and correction from having been involved in a horribly destructive group, sometimes for many years. An enlightened subgroup of the body of Christ that knows something about this condition and the dangers of short–circuiting the therapeutic process with clichés and instant–cure concepts can be very helpful. Nevertheless, all of us, and particularly these people, are engaged in spiritual warfare, and the ultimate victory does come through the grace and power of Jesus Christ.

Please refer to *Beyond the Darkness* to obtain more information about ritual abuse, dissociation and its effects of depersonalization and derealization, multiple personality disorder (which should always be suspected in cases of ritualistic sexual abuse), and treatment of ritual sexual abuse.

IN DARKNESS AND PAIN—
EFFECTS OF SEXUAL ABUSE

In the aftermath of sexual abuse, you will find that even in your day–to–day problems, its effects can be far reaching.

These effects include rage and depression, hatred, low self–esteem, self–destructive behavior (Note: Some persons reflect self–hate and painful emotions by cutting and burning themselves. Others may engage in dangerous behavior such as shoplifting or driving recklessly.), memory blocks, perfectionism, betrayal, fear, and repeated victimization. With your counselor's help, you will find that identifying the effects that have occurred in your life will provide a framework for developing specific goals in your recovery and direction for your prayers.

A list of The Overcomer's Hopes is included here to give you encouragement because looking at the effects of sexual abuse in your life may temporarily overwhelm you. As you read these hopes, understand that they are also promises that God can bring to pass. At times you will get discouraged in your recovery process; when you do, take several moments to read these promises.

The Overcomer's Hope

In Christ I can:
1) live a life without fear controlling me.
2) live a life without being controlled by others.
3) live a life without condemnation or condemning others.
4) live a life without shame and guilt.
5) live a life where I know the difference between what is safe and what is not safe.
6) live a life without rage, hate, and depression.
7) live a life with stable emotions.
8) live a life with joy and happiness—even in the midst of trials.
9) live a life with peace and love.
10) live a life without helplessness.
11) live a life with appropriate sexual behavior.
12) live a life understanding my value in Christ.
13) live a life where I can be intimate with others.
14) live a life where I can trust others who are trustworthy.
15) live a life where I have a deep relationship with God.

THE FAMILY IN DARKNESS— RELATIONSHIPS AND RESPONSIBILITY

Learning to understand the role your family played in your sexual abuse is essential to your recovery.

In most of the families where sexual abuse occurs, the families are decidedly dysfunctional, that is, unable to meet the God–given needs for nurturing in a family system. A family in which the father is the perpetrator may also include a mother who is a passive co–perpetrator; an uncle could be the perpetrator while both parents are co–perpetrators. In families where the child is abused by a baby–sitter, the child, as we would expect, has been told to obey the sitter. In all these cases, since the child believes the parents must know what is going on, he/she has a great deal of anger toward both parents.

Other dysfunctional families could include one in which a child who has been raped cannot disclose the fact because the entire family is emotionally shut down and incapable of giving support; it could be a single–parent family with mother as head of the household and children cared for by a baby–sitter, left alone, or in the presence of strangers more often than other children, thus increasing the chances for victimization; a family in which alcohol or drugs are abused; a family in which role–reversal occurs and children must play adult to their parents' child figure, taking responsibility for making everything all right, but frustrated by not knowing how to make that happen; an authoritative family system, usually dominated by the father who has a submissive wife. One young woman in such a family was sexually abused by her domineering, scripture–quoting father, who also abused her two other sisters. She found it almost impossible to believe in a loving God called "Father."

Victims of abuse may also have lived with more than one family, perhaps first with mother and father, next with grandmother and grandfather, then in foster homes, each presenting different challenges for recovery. Dealing with emotional abuse, chaos, and the aftermath of sexual abuse would implant a profound feeling of inadequacy in a person unable to change, alter, or control such instability.

Each family member sends us messages about ourselves. The parent or sibling who perpetrates sexual abuse says, *You're worthless. You are no good and you are guilty*. The same message, can be sent by words and attitudes. *Don't express your feelings; Don't cry, Don't get upset, Don't get angry; Don't betray the family, Don't ever tell outsiders about the family secrets*. These messages, as well as others more directly stated, affect recovery, particularly those that say you are no good, that you are a failure, or that place shame on you.

By contrast, building a healthy self–image in a child, an adult, or in a recovering sexual abuse victim requires everyday reinforcement of that person's value, not only in positive statements but also in physical contact. The part played by touching has recently received considerable attention, especially bonding between infant and mother and father. Unfortunately, in a family in darkness, the only touching may have been bad touching, rather than the normal healthy physical love God created us to express through such gestures as hugging, holding hands, and kissing.

Working through these family issues is painful and will probably continue to be so throughout recovery for the person in a dysfunctional family. Those who feel desolate, betrayed, and alone, need to reach out to someone who can help. Joining a sexual abuse overcomers' group, or beginning individual counseling can help break the feeling of shame over having been abused. However recovery is pursued, it is most important for survivors to receive the support God wants to provide for overcoming this tragedy. It is his intention for you to walk in joy and peace, free from guilt and condemnation.

Allowing God to become closest family—placing Him at the center of your life—will give you the family support, the family love and the family unit you did not have.

It is important to allow God also to replace your feelings of unworthiness with his facts about your worthiness, to transform your hopelessness into hope in Christ and your profound feelings of inadequacy into adequacy found only in Him. You are deeply loved by Him, fully pleasing to Him, and totally accepted by Him. You are totally acceptable.

Allow God to restore to you all that was taken by your family, to nurture you, to comfort you, and to encourage you. Trust God to love you even if no one else has ever loved you.

Each day for twenty–two days, read the entire list of messages that follow, and also read and meditate on a different one of the accompanying scriptures each day.

Scripture reference	God's Messages to You as a Believer
Genesis 1:26–27	I am uniquely created in God's image.
Matthew 5:13	I am the salt of the earth.
Matthew 5:14	I am the light of the world.
Luke 11:9–10	I ask and receive; I seek and find; I knock and the door is opened unto me.
John 8:32	The truth has set me free.
John 14:27	I have peace.
John 17:18	I have been sent into the world.
John 17:22	I have God's glory.
Acts 13:38	I have forgiveness of sins through Christ.
Romans 8:1	I have now no condemnation.
Romans 8:32	I have all things.
Romans 12:6	I have been given gifts.
1 Corinthians 2:16	I have the mind of Christ.
1 Corinthians 3:9	I am God's fellow–worker; I am God's field, God's building.
2 Corinthians 4:16	I am being renewed day by day.
Ephesians 3:20	I have a power source within me which is able to do exceeding abundantly beyond all that I ask or think.
Philippians 4:7	The peace of God guards my heart and mind.
Philippians 4:13	I can do all things through Him who strengthens me.
Philippians 4:19	God shall supply all my needs according to His riches in glory in Christ Jesus.
2 Timothy 1:7	For God has not given me a spirit of timidity, but of power and love and discipline.
Philemon 6	The knowledge of every good thing is in me.
1 Peter 2:9–10	I am chosen.

BELIEVING THE DARKNESS— LIES VERSUS TRUTHS

The experience of being sexually abused almost always leaves its victims with a very damaging set of false beliefs. They learn to base their reactions to people and situations upon those misconceptions and if they must look to a dysfunctional family system for support, they will only find more anguish and pain.

Further effects of living a life based on false beliefs include: 1) the inability to enjoy healthy sexual interaction with one's spouse; 2) the inability to express healthy affection with one's children, and 3) a dependence on having needs met through sexual interaction, addiction, or promiscuity.

Still other problems derive from feelings of guilt and abuse, leading victims to think of themselves as dirty or undeserving of respect and setting them up to be revictimized. Suicidal thoughts are not uncommon.

Sexually molested children often suffer delayed or even incomplete physical and mental maturation. Rather than knowing themselves to be loved and valuable human beings, they must try to mature in life from a foundation based in confusion and betrayal. Almost inevitably they reach adulthood in a state of emotional instability.

Sexually molested children commonly believe 1) that the abuse is their fault, 2) that adults can do no wrong, or 3) that they desired the sexual activity. In the first case, the perpetrator establishes in children's minds the concept of "we." "We" are doing this; therefore "we" are responsible. As they grow older, this concept of "we" becomes more firmly cemented in their minds. Thinking of all the times they could have asked the abuser to stop but didn't, they accept total responsibility for the abuse. The reality is that a child rarely, if ever, could have gotten it stopped.

Second, even when children do think of an adult as having done something bad, they still feel as if they made the adult do it. The question of a child's having "wanted it" places unwarranted guilt for having had a normal physiological reaction to stimulation. God created the human body for healthy sexual interaction, and it is the perpetrator who has misused that gift.

The most common, and devastating, false beliefs are those causing feelings of low self—worth. Any statements we or others make that label us "no good," "a failure," "stupid," "ugly," and the like, when repeated often enough, are accepted as truths and eventually acted out.

Perpetrators, by taking what they want from their victims, not only send the message that their victims have no real value but that there are no boundaries, an idea particularly harmful to children, who are not yet mature enough to understand boundaries and thus are often set up to be revictimized. Repeated victimization firmly fixes the idea of worthlessness in the mind of the victim, regardless of age.

A significant problem for sexually abused children is lack of parental reaction to their attempts to disclose. Most victims are violated by someone they know, most commonly a significant other, such as a father or stepfather. Unfortunately, the parent or significant other whom they try to tell may not always recognize that the child wants to disclose a problem. In addition, parents are particularly likely not to want to believe that a spouse is engaging in such destructive behavior. To complicate the situation even more, children often attempt to disclose bad things that are happening to them through their behavior rather than simply by telling someone about it. These signs include sexual behavior inappropriate for their age, sudden unruly behavior, falling grades, stealing, or some form of self–abuse. If no one picks up on children's attempted disclosures, verbal or behavioral, they begin to feel that no one cares what is happening, and if no one cares, the idea that he or she must truly be worthless is reinforced. Validation of what the victim has said thus is particularly important. If children sense anger and/or a nonsupportive attitude from the person(s) they have told, they may recant or not be willing to risk completing the disclosure they most likely have not fully revealed. In most cases, children have not lied; they are only trying to avoid trouble.

It is crucial for victims to understand the origin of their faulty beliefs and to begin correcting them so that the self–perpetuating destructive effects of those beliefs do not continue. If whatever you are thinking about yourself has been distorted by sexual abuse, determine not to agree with those thoughts or statements. God's message is, *You're not worthless, you are special!* and He wants you to develop the skill of standing up and saying that for yourself.

Five important steps that can help put you on the road to recovery are:
1. Identify the false beliefs that are blocking your path.
2. Look for the roots of these false beliefs and the underlying factors that are causing you to maintain them.

3. Recognize and accept these false beliefs as lies, and totally and finally relinquish them.
4. Pray to God that he will wither away your false beliefs and reaffirm to you His truth about you.
5. Use God's word, the Bible, to set you free from the deception of all the destructive falsehoods that have been holding you in their grip. Learn to take a stand, even argue against yourself in order to develop a true belief system not rooted and grounded in sexual abuse. Learn not to be so harsh and critical of yourself, but rather to love yourself.

As further aid, make this Prayer for Perseverance a daily affirmation:

Thank you for making me a prized treasure with a special plan for my life. Thank you that you have equipped me with everything that I need to achieve the goal that has been set before me. Thank you, Lord, that when I stumble, You lift me up; when I try to run away, You come after me; when I am defeated, You cause me to persevere to triumph. Thank you, Lord, for your perfect love for me.

THE DARKNESS AND THE LIGHT— RESPONSIBILITY, BETRAYAL, AND DENIAL

Every victim must deal with the issues of responsibility, betrayal, and denial. First, each victim must give *total responsibility to the abuser*. Obstacles to taking that important step are confusion, loss of objectivity, and loss of normal reasoning abilities. Many rape victims take the responsibility, at least in part, for the rape ... if she just hadn't gone to the party ...; if she just hadn't left fifteen minutes late from work and had to take the second bus ... she might not have been a victim. But someone would have been.

Victims must begin to understand that they were victims. *Webster's New College Dictionary* defines *victim* as "one who is injured, destroyed, or sacrificed under any of various conditions," including rage, ambition, etc. Responsibility for the abuse must be placed upon the abuser, not upon the victim.

Sometimes victims received so–called "benefits" from the abuser, an argument that asks that the victim pay for normal demonstrations of affection in family relationships. A father–daughter relationship should include good times, presents, and love; not a role reversal between mother and daughter, and certainly not sex.

The victim also must give responsibility to any co–perpetrator, that is, any individual who knowingly aids or allows the perpetrator to perform an abusive act. A mother's responsibility as a co–perpetrator must be recognized and dealt with if she fails to fulfill her normal role of "taking care of her kids" (although the victim has to consider whether mother really knows of any abuse).

Most co–perpetrators are guilty of sins of omission rather than commission. Many noticed little things that weren't quite right, but ignored or discounted what they saw or felt was happening.

Other primary caretakers may have been too busy or too troubled, or may have been victims themselves. The point is for the victim to acknowledge that others were responsible and to give that responsibility to all who should or could have been accountable.

Among other pieces to the problem are our society's attitudes toward women, children, sex, and pornography, as well as the question of God's responsibility in permitting such evils. The strongest argument concerning the latter is that in God's master plan he wants a true love relationship with His children, which can only come about if they have free will to love Him or reject Him. Victims are often betrayed by the effects of sexual abuse, seduced into an undesirable lifestyle. Children in need of a healthy relationship with a parent are abandoned in the world of incest.

Victims of abuse often deny the abuse, actually lying to themselves. Usually they have detached themselves from their feelings. As young victims or older victims, in the violent crimes of rape and incest, they shut down, as often happens after the shock of physical trauma. Understandably, the shutdown is emotional as well as physical. The protective overload devices of body and mind, however, are intended for temporary use only; the longer they remain in place, the more damage they do.

If you are a victim of sexual abuse, but in denial, it is time to come out of that state, give responsibility to the perpetrator, accept your betrayal, and begin the process of dealing with very painful memories. The process of healing has many ups and downs and proceeds at varying rates, but can only take place after you begin. If memories and feelings become too hurtful or tend to promote destructive behavior, back off and rest. Once you are stabilized, you may safely resume the process.

Beware of using denial because of the idea that the truth must be avoided since Christians are supposed to have forgiven their enemies and to be victorious. Until a victim of sexual abuse begins to deal with the truth there is no hope of healing.

BEYOND THE DARKNESS—
PRINCIPLES OF RESTORATION

It is important for survivors of sexual abuse to understand the Biblical principles of restoration. The meaning of one of the Hebrew words for restoration, "to live," provides a helpful image for victims of abuse, who have suffered a mental and emotional death. Restoration means that finally, perhaps for the first time in their lives, they are fully alive.

Psalm 23 is a powerful chapter for restoration from abuse, particularly for victims who can't relate to God as Father. Reading Psalm 23 five times a day for one week will help change a distorted attitude about God, particularly that of viewing God as a remote, all–powerful judge rather than as the shepherd who lovingly cares for his sheep.

God not only restores His children to life, but even to the former state of being that was taken from them by the perpetrator. Many victims have had part or all of their childhood stolen. Begin your restoration now by risking and believing that God will restore the life that has been stolen from you.

The Twelve Steps to Restoration from Sexual Abuse that follow are essential to your recovery:

1. Acknowledge that you have been sexually abused and identify the effects that the abuse is having in your life.
2. Return the responsibility for your abuse to the perpetrator, co–perpetrator, family system, and/or any other contributing sources.
3. Acknowledge God as the source and power of restoration. Know that God is not the source of abuse but the solution to the trauma of that abuse.
4. Recount each experience of abuse by writing, talking, and sharing, again and again until the pain is gone.
5. Pray daily for restoration from the sexual abuse, the passive abuse, the physical abuse, the emotional abuse, and the verbal abuse.
6. Work through denial, anger, guilt, shame, fear, betrayal, hurt, and loneliness, and learn to express your emotions and feelings.
7. Grieve over the suffering caused by all the things that were done to you and all the things you were forced to do. Grieve and

release the pent–up rage at the lack of support and love that should have been there for you.

8. Fix your worth, value, and esteem in the Word of God. Resist all guilt–producing, destructive messages from the world and Satan. Find your significance in God.

9. Commit yourself to the biblical principle of forgiveness, and send away all hurts, despair, and agony of your abuse.

10. Allow God to cause your pain to be forgotten one day at a time, one memory at a time.

11. With the support and guidance of a professional, decide whether or not to confront the perpetrator and other responsible persons. If direct confrontation is not advisable, express your feelings in a letter which may or may not be mailed after discussing it with your counselor.

12. Accept the fact that restoration will take time, but don't despair. Trust, peace, love, and wholeness will be yours. You have survived sexual abuse. Now overcome your trauma and go beyond the darkness.

SHARING THE DARKNESS— DEALING WITH SHAME AND GUILT

Every victim of sexual abuse is challenged by the need to recover from the shame and the guilt resulting from the experience. The shame is the individual's feeling of humiliating disgrace at having been the victim of sexual abuse, while guilt is her or his terrible burden of "knowing" he or she has committed some great offense. In the process of recovery, the victim must give back the shame to the perpetrator and erase the false sentence of guilt.

The initial disclosure is perhaps the most difficult challenge of the entire recovery process. Many victims have been threatened emotionally and physically or shamed into believing that terrible things would happen to them or to someone close to them if they were to tell. Secrecy gives shame and guilt the power to torment victims and isolates victims by

33

making them believe they are the only ones experiencing such upsetting trauma.

Telling the story in a safe environment dilutes and destroys the strength of the memories of the abuse. As those memories are shared, they lose their power to nourish shame and guilt.

The kind of toxic guilt and shame experienced in sexual abuse does not lead to godly conviction, repentance, and acceptance, but rather, to condemnation. A helpful plan may be to quote Romans 8:1, "There is therefore now no condemnation to them which are in Christ Jesus," every time a harmful memory comes to mind, then jot down a note to tell this memory to someone. Eventually the flashbacks should become less frequent, until they are gone altogether.

Guilt is embedded in the feelings of inadequacy experienced during sexual abuse. These feelings are further reinforced by the repetition of messages that say *you are not equal* or *you are not worth as much as I am*, and *my needs are more important than yours*.

Guilt often produces anger turned inward and leads to depression. To combat this and other devastating effects of guilt, examine as objectively as you can those areas in which you feel guilty. Relinquish these areas of your life again and again to God. Depend on Him to be faithful and just, and also good. Allow God to overcome all thoughts of guilt—deserved and undeserved—through His goodness; His path of freedom will be more than worth the effort.

Webster's New Collegiate Dictionary defines shame as "a painful emotion excited by a consciousness of guilt, shortcoming, or impropriety; disgrace, dishonor." The shame message of sexual abuse comes from three major areas: 1) the perpetrator and the denigration of the abuse; 2) false personal feelings about the body and body parts; and 3) neglect and disdain by others. All messages that convey worthlessness are shame messages that will only be alleviated by learning to speak God's word about yourself, not the perpetrator's damaging words about you. One's own hate toward the body or toward the mind can be transformed by Jesus: "And do not be conformed to this world, but be transformed by the renewing of your mind [do not believe the message of shame, but rather God's wisdom], that you may prove what the will of God is, that which is good and acceptable and perfect" (Romans 12:2). In other words, begin to understand that as Christ works healing, the abuse can no longer continue to haunt you.

Feeling the Darkness—Anger and Hurt

All victims have anger and need to learn to express it appropriately. That does not mean blowing up, throwing things, or using any form of violence; it does mean acknowledging, accepting, and expressing anger in nonviolent, biblical ways.

Persons unable to restrain themselves from expressing anger by harming others should immediately seek the help of a professional. They should also try to recognize and eliminate any behavior patterns that have been learned from being around angry people and be alert to the possibility that lack of proper rest, physical disabilities, or improper diet could be aggravating their anger.

Once victims have taken the necessary step of giving themselves permission to be angry, the challenge is to give appropriate outward expression to their inner anger toward every perpetrator and co–perpetrator. Anger should not be taken out on oneself or others who are not involved.

Begin by making a list of everyone with whom you are angry concerning your abuse. Include everyone from the actual perpetrator to all the co–perpetrators, remembering that a perpetrator is anyone who has sexually abused you in any way and a co–perpetrator is anyone who, by omission or commission, allowed the abuse to happen. Co–perpetrators can include parents, siblings, teachers, pastors, protective services, and even the legal system. Do not omit one person, system, or organization when making your list of those with whom you are angry. Don't be afraid to include yourself and God, but don't misdirect anger toward those not involved or toward yourself alone.

We become angry when we have been rejected, humiliated, or used, or when we have been hurt mentally, physically, or emotionally.

We can make one of three choices to deal with anger: 1) turn it to the outside and blame everyone for all the bad things that have happened to us; 2) turn it inside and blame ourselves for everything bad that has happened to us (either of these two choices will eventually lead to emotional destruction); or 3) learn to express our anger using God–given biblical principles. Clearly the third choice is best for our emotional and spiritual health.

The time of recovery is one in which victims can and should express anger. Anger is an ally, but not a helpful one when characterized as a silent rage inside. The effects of unexpressed anger in a person who has been sexually abused can take the form of chronic anxiety, eating disorder, multiple personality disorder, depression, promiscuity, alcoholism, and a host of other problems.

Anger may at first have seemed to help many survive abuse and keep going, but the time comes to grieve over the hurt and direct the anger appropriately. A support group for sexual abuse survivors under individual therapy is probably the best solution, but if this is impossible, someone should be found who can help you process the pain of your trauma, preferably someone who understands the issues of sexual abuse.

If there is absolutely no one, there is God. Even though it may appear to a victim that He was not there at the time of abuse, He was. He was sad and angry over the abuse. Nobody wants justice more than God. Please reach out to Him and allow Him to touch you and to help you.

As a major step to recovery, after you acknowledge your hurt, take the list of perpetrators and co–perpetrators you have made and write each of those persons, organizations, or systems a letter that you do not mail. Letters to the deceased may be written as good–by letters or written to Jesus, asking Him to deliver the message.

Read these letters to a group, a trusted individual, or an empty chair. Then, write God a letter expressing your anger.

As anger is processed in one area, God may bring additional issues to mind. Accept the challenge. Express yourself honestly and allow your anger to be a healthy part of your life. Reading the Psalms may help accomplish this important step, particularly the ones that cry out, "Come quickly," "How long, O God, will you turn from me?" and so on. Vent your pent–up feelings; recount mistakes made as an adult, whether a result of the abuse or not; express your anger toward yourself until you can really believe in Romans 8:1: "Therefore, there is now no condemnation to those in Christ Jesus." Finally, as your anger is dissipated, you should be able to accept yourself.

LIVING IN THE DARKNESS— HEALING LONELINESS AND FEAR

It is almost impossible to describe the loneliness of abuse...the terror, the despair, the desolation of the nights and days...the forsakenness...the horror of dwelling in darkness. Many victims have a great fear of their perpetrators, and every effort needs to be taken to protect these victims. Fear of perpetrators may require a long recovery process. For example, an 11–year–old girl who was anally, orally, and vaginally raped by three male perpetrators has needed more than three years just to overcome her fear of men.

Every victim's story includes fears, some very rational and others not. Wisdom and general respect for the reality of life circumstances is certainly necessary. For example, being wary of jogging alone at 10 o'clock at night in a major U.S. city could hardly be considered an irrational fear. But, if someone is afraid to take a desirable job in a reputable area across town, that person needs to discover whether it is simply that the job is inconveniently far from home, or whether there are deeper fears to be overcome. This can be accomplished through telling one's story and sharing feelings with a counselor, a recovery group, or a meaningful friend, and by all means, claiming God's redeeming, healing promises.

There are many ways of trying to compensate for our loneliness and our fears: minimizing or denying the problem; trying to win approval by doing everything for everyone; attempting to be perfect, with a perfect home, perfect child and perfect spouse; maintaining constant anger toward everyone and everybody; engaging in daredevil behavior such as skydiving or racing; overindulging in eating, shopping, or volunteer work.

But no matter what the compensation may be, only God's plan will work. He is the deliverer and restorer. We will progress in recovery when we face our fears and loneliness by telling our story to appropriate others and releasing those burdens to God.

To overcome loneliness, start by acknowledging each lonely feeling, one by one, and handing it to God. Do the same with all the ways you've compensated for those lonely feelings and the ways you've survived one more day. Pray again Psalm 51:6, asking God to reveal the truth of your loneliness, even though this process may be painful. Submit your irrational fears to Him, one at a time, and receive His restoration from abusive situations. Seek and accept accurate information rather than continue in faulty beliefs.

In the spiritual area, in which strong feelings of a presence of evil may be felt, seek the "spirit of power and love and a sound mind" referred to in 2 Timothy 1:7.

Most victims must process the fear of abandonment. Fears for personal safety are very real to children, although they may seem groundless to an adult. Adult victims at times do not remember or recognize the fears related to their sexual abuse, often experiencing them indirectly, unspecifically, and unexpectedly, as in sleep problems, anxiety hysteria, fears of thunderstorms, elevators, and other phobias. When we are in fear, we are in bondage to the thoughts and actions we think will gain us peace. It does no good to run away from fear, ignore it, or try to compensate for it. We must seek competent help and use the Word of God and the comfort of His people.

Individuals who are in too much pain or fear to do anything may be helped by memorizing such short scriptures as Matthew 11:28, James 4:7, and 2 Samuel 22:2, and recalling them when support is needed. Praying the Lord's Prayer every day and applying the words *but deliver us from evil* to specific fears will also help.

No one loses the reality of past loneliness and abandonment, but in the recovery process God redeems the time spent in that condition, filling the present with His love, joy, and peace. First Corinthians 13:4–8a provides great comfort. First read it as is; then read it again, replacing the word *love* with the word *God*. After that, read it a third time with the word *I* instead of the word *love*. In the recovery process remember that God *is* love. God never fails; love never fails. He will never abandon us.

OVERCOMING THE DARKNESS—
ISSUES OF TRUST AND CONTROL

From the moment we were born, all of us were meant to have trust firmly established in our minds and hearts by parents and other significant individuals, but victims of abuse, especially of childhood incest, have had the very core of trust plucked from them. Children who have been abused by a non–family member and who have a healthy, nurturing family can somewhat more quickly respond to the right intervention, but victims who come from unstable and unreliable families face an immense challenge in developing the ability and faith to trust.

Our standard English dictionaries list among their definitions of *trust* "to rely upon or place confidence in someone or something"; and "to place hope in someone or something; to expect confidently"; "to take shelter in a safe place." Sexual abuse victims learn only too well not to have hope in or confident expectation of someone, that there is no place to flee to, that you must survive by yourself, and that no one is there for you. They learn to survive, usually alone. Many victims believe that people in general are instruments of cruelty and thus avoid them. But God created us to be in communion with other humans and with Him. The tragedy is that victims who are unable to trust in God are rejecting the very One who can save them from the effects of their abuse and teach them to trust the right people. He is their refuge—the place to flee to.

Sexual abuse distorts understanding. As compensation for the inability to trust and feel secure without fear, victims try to control their lives by accumulating money and power and controlling other people, or by isolating themselves, rationalizing, avoiding people, running away, suspecting all others and checking everything out. Even when they fail, they keep on trying to control rather than risk trusting. The irony is that the more we attempt to control, the more we will be controlled; the more we attempt to control our circumstances, the more our circumstances will control us.

Christian counseling provides a haven to which victims can go and learn again to trust, and where individuals can be loved for who they are. Eventually, as the Lord continues to work in their lives, they begin to feel safe in other places and with other people.

Some people, for a period of time, are successful at controlling their environment, but eventually this fails because it takes so much energy. To deny the pain of abuse takes still more energy. Pushed down, negative emotions eventually emerge as physical, emotional, or behavioral problems.

Learning to trust *is* the road to recovery. At first, attempt to trust God in small areas and at the same time, to trust yourself. Recognize that even though it may seem God is too late to help, He will get you through your ordeal. As you learn to trust God completely, even when things happen that you don't like, you will find you can trust some people for certain things and others more completely. There is no need to control people or to keep them at a distance. You do need people, and that is good and not bad; God made us all to need each other.

Determine what areas you are trying to dominate in your life. It is often difficult to recognize the clues, especially if the area of control is an integral part of your personality or job responsibility. For instance, question whether rigid organization in your daily life means you are simply being neat and punctual or whether you are controlling others by forcing them to do everything a certain way and at a certain time; or whether you genuinely like to do generous things for others or are controlling them by making them feel guilty at accepting so much from you.

Develop a healthy awareness for the appropriate placement of trust. Since sexual abuse so often produces clouded vision in its victims, it is very important to pray for the ability to discern, to understand and to know, to recognize good and evil and to see the results of both. We need to hear the truth and to sense deception. We can also learn from the experience of being in a group or counseling situation where openness and trust are modeled.

A final definition for *trust* is "to expect confidently; to wait." To trust is to do what God expects of you, and many times He requires waiting. There will be a day, even when you sin, even when you are betrayed, even when you feel God is too late, that you will be like the Psalmist who cast himself upon God and God delivered him (Ps. 22:24). Trust God and let Him deliver you from all your fears, all your needs to control. Let Him teach you to trust that which is trustworthy.

FORGETTING THE DARKNESS— THE PROCESS OF FORGIVENESS

Without forgiveness, you cannot walk in the wholeness God has for you.

Until there has been time to process all the difficult pain of abuse, the very mention of forgiveness will seem unthinkable. Unreleased anger must still be expressed, and denial in an area of pain must be overcome. Perhaps you still believe that if you forgive the perpetrator, he is forgiven by God and is no longer accountable to God for the sin.

There is no mandate from God that says you must forgive your offender immediately after the offense. You don't have to. You can forgive when you are ready. Not wanting to forgive is a normal reaction to severe offenses. This chapter is simply the presentation of His principles of forgiveness, and it will only be through God that you can eventually be motivated to take this step.

There are several reasons why we may not want to forgive.

1. *We may be too angry, too hurt, or too afraid, and believe that unforgiveness will protect us from being hurt again.* Inevitably the opposite occurs, and the offense continues to affect us as the pain turns into rage and bitterness.

2. *We may think that forgiving somehow gives the person permission to hurt us again.* Forgiving someone does not give that person permission to hurt us again, even if that does happen.

3. *We believe unforgiveness will somehow hurt the perpetrator, but the opposite is true.* Perpetrators, unforgiven, go right on doing what they want to do. They never considered their victims in the first place, and our unforgiveness has absolutely no effect on their behavior.

4. *The offense is too great.* In *The Search For Significance*,* Robert McGee states this as one of several reasons individuals do not forgive. But despite the great offense of sexual abuse, for our own complete recovery we must let go of it and of the offender. It harms only us to refuse to forgive the perpetrator, the co–perpetrator, and anyone or anything else that would impede us from our goal.

* Robert S. McGee, *The Search for Significance*, 2d ed. (Houston, TX: Rapha Publishing, 1990), p. 122.

5. *The perpetrator never apologized*. The victim may want to forgive the perpetrator, but his or her failure to admit being sorry simply deepens the anger at the offense.

6. *The perpetrator committed the abuse deliberately and repeatedly*. The problem for the victim here is in trying to make sense of the abuse. If it had been without forethought or deliberation, forgiveness might have seemed easier. Yet, if we were to base our forgiveness on forgiving only accidental sin, we probably wouldn't be able to forgive very much.

7. *There was no abuse*. Most perpetrators, when confronted, deny any abuse, arguing that what they did was the victim's fault and that the experience was a good one for the victim, or that the victim really wanted it.

Some victims don't forgive the perpetrators, they rationalize; that is, they continue to deny their own feelings in the forgiveness process and thus offer the perpetrator cheap grace: "I must forgive because I am a child of God"; "he (or she) had a really bad childhood"; or "I feel really sorry for him (her), since I found out about his (her) life." The problem with this logic is that it is rationalization, not forgiveness. We may feel very sorry for someone whose early years had been marred by bad circumstances, but that background doesn't give permission to rape or commit any other sin. Many thousands of people with such childhoods choose to find a more productive way to live their lives than sexually abusing someone.

Victims are particularly prone to rationalize about the co–perpetrator's role. Regardless of how innocent the co–perpetrator may seem, it is nevertheless important, for the victim to forgive him or her and allow that memory fragment to resurface.

Victims who have a codependency problem typically display a lack of objectivity and feeling of overresponsibility for the abuse and are truly unable to implement the principle of forgiveness. The codependent victim may not feel either free or responsible to forgive because of the role reversal in which he or she has exchanged places with the co–perpetrator.and is thus not the victim. Additionally, this same codependent victim may think it unnecessary to forgive because of being partly responsible (in her exchanged role) for the abuse. For a detailed discussion of the pitfalls to codependent behavior, see Pat Springle's book, *Codependency*.*

Forgiveness, however, does have a great impact on our lives. Forgiving, for the victim, could mean sending away the hurt, the anger, the bitterness, the sadness, and, most important, the abuse. At some point, we must recognize that the forgiveness we may grant is really for

* Pat Springle, *Codependency* 2d ed. (Houston, TX: Rapha Publishing, 1990).

us. Our unforgiveness holds us in bondage to the pain of the abuse. Certainly our forgiving of the perpetrator affects our responses and relationship to him or her, but the perpetrator is not wholly forgiven unless he or she goes before God and personally seeks His forgiveness.

Forgiveness confronts the victim with a difficult challenge, but unforgiveness will create a multitude of problems, including re-living again and again the memories of the sexual abuse. When we don't forgive and allow God to restore His love back to us, we risk walking in bitterness and despair as we feel the force of unforgiveness through stress, turmoil, and horrible memories.

For every victim, to forgive is a decision. Typically, the process is one that requires a long period of time since it is not likely to be a one-time event but one that is repeated over and over.

Recovery is between the victim and God, yet God does not offer the option of unforgiveness. The Lord's Prayer clearly asks that we forgive others who sin against us, as the Father forgives us for our sins against Him. If someone sins against me or if I sin, something has been lost to me. Sin takes and God gives. God gives restoration as a by-product of forgiveness.

Don't be dismayed if you're not ready to forgive. God will help you to get there. Pray for restoration and that God will truly cause the pain to be forgotten. When you can make a decision to forgive and you can trust what God says even just a little, He will restore you.

DESTROYING THE DARKNESS— INTIMACY IN RELATIONSHIPS

Victims struggle greatly with the issue of intimacy. God–given needs for intimacy are and were always a part of them, but were never met in a healthy way or with any consistency. Every boundary of *intimacy* was violated by the sexual abuse. Victims are afraid of putting deep trust in anyone lest they be betrayed again. However, most are too lonely and afraid to be independent from others. This dilemma is often overwhelming, as they hunger for intimacy like an unfed child hungers for food.

Webster's Dictionary describes intimacy as "belonging to one's deepest nature; marked by a very close association with someone else; friendship that is marked by warmness and a long association; a very personal and private association with another individual."

Intimacy is freedom; the ability to set and maintain boundaries, to disclose personal and private matters when and if you choose, to trust those who are trustworthy and to form long–term, meaningful relationships with others who desire intimacy as well. Intimacy is the deepest commitment of love and the deepest expression of love. In the journey toward restoration and recovery, intimacy will be found, and it will destroy the darkness and the trauma of the abuse.

Victims who are single have unique problems in their need for intimacy. Because of being alone, there is less opportunity for them to develop the ability to achieve intimacy, and at the same time far more opportunity to retreat into isolation and depression. Vulnerability to attack is greater, and the need for support in recovery does not have the resource of a caring spouse.

Joining a sexual abuse group, if you are not already taking part in one, is a good way to work toward the ability to achieve intimacy. Its environment provides a safe place for taking the risk of being more open.

Past neglect and abandonment have a profound effect on the ability to achieve intimacy. Victims who have experienced neglect will need to pray for restoration again and again until they feel safe. Talking, writing, and expressing feelings with supportive people will increase the ability to share the private and personal things of their lives, and also the ability to ask for private and personal needs to be met.

Victims of neglect will be helped by praying specifically for all areas that they know are keeping them from risking themselves in relationships, especially self–hate. Many victims of all kinds of abuse despise themselves and find it very difficult to receive concern and affection from others, or to believe that someone could really love them. A second major step is for them to begin to believe in themselves, and know that God believes in them.

A declaration which Rapha clients are asked to read once every morning and evening helps them understand who they really are in Christ as it affirms their worth with supportive scriptures. This entire declaration can be found in *Beyond the Darkness* and in other resource materials available through Rapha Publishing, 8876 Gulf Freeway, Suite 340, Houston, TX 77017.

It will be helpful to review the following list of probable causes for emotional isolation, and to pray for specific understanding of how any of these causes have had an impact on your ability to be intimate.

Probable Causes for Emotional Isolation

Sexual abuse	Shame
Poor self–image	Guilt
Family messages	Fear
Abandonment	Depression
Neglect	Inability to trust

When we react to any of the items in the foregoing list by isolating ourselves emotionally, we risk failure in having our intimacy needs met. Self–pity, anger, hardness of heart, overcritical judgmentalism, perfectionism, false compassion, attention–demanding behavior, compulsive behavior, denial, indulgence in fantasy, and unforgiveness are among the attitudes we adopt. A look at the following list of behavioral tendencies (see *Beyond the Darkness* for an expanded list), coupled with the ensuing discussion of the reactions named here, clearly challenges us at this point in our recovery process.

Reasons for Inability to Form Successful Intimate Relationships

Persons who have been sexually abused may:

1) tend to become immobilized by romantic obsessions.
2) send a double message of wanting another person to show affection, and rejecting affection that is offered
3) search for some magical quality in another person that will make them feel complete
4) take themselves too seriously and be unable to joke with others
5) use sex to feel validated and complete
6) be too critical of partners and of self; may interpret simple misunderstandings in the relationship as betrayal
7) be suspicious and constantly test people in relationships
8) constantly seek intimacy with another person; may be desperate for intimacy but unable to be intimate

Anger must be dealt with appropriately and not allowed to lead to resentment, bitterness, or retaliation, nor should it become a barrier to intimacy. We must learn to get past our anger and see things in perspective, not judging people based on one incident or on the past.

Putting a shell around ourselves through hardness of heart or resorting to bullying others will only increase pain and loneliness.

Being critical of others, constantly standing in judgment of others and setting unrealistic standards, assures that we do not have to get too close, because no one will be able to measure up.

Demanding attention, acting like clowns or show–offs, or adopting extreme dress and loud personalities do not meet intimacy needs, and often lead to rejection.

Compensating for intimacy needs with some type of compulsive behavior that "feels good" (eating, smoking, drinking, spending money, engaging in promiscuity, etc.) or accumulating material things may make us feel better temporarily, but cannot fill the need for close relationships. Some victims give in to sexual lust and must have someone there to hold, to sleep with, and to have sex with. Often this leads to being revictimized or to sexual addictions. Suppressing the need for intimacy simply doesn't work.

An area of intimacy that sexual abuse commonly destroys is that of sexual relations in a marriage. Victims confide that they never had a problem with sex until they got married. Some who were sexually active before marriage wonder if God is punishing them now in their marriage. He is not: marriage after abuse appears to present the same problems for the victim as the abusive situation did, in that victims feel that they "have to" engage in sex. Consciously or unconsciously, they feel their power of choice once again has been taken from them.

Many times victims have flashbacks while having intercourse with their spouse. If spouses do something similar to what the abuser did, victims will be unable to respond. Sometimes, before starting in recovery, victims have been spared the common problem of dysfunction in the sexual area of their marriage. But during the recovery process, they may no longer desire to have sex with their partners because of emerging painful memories. All of these things are normal for victims and can be worked through with two committed, Christian partners. The counseling professional may even advise the couple to abstain from sex for a period of time, but be assured that recovery will work.

Certainly the most physically intimate thing each of us does with another person is to have sexual relations. We uncover our bodies and leave ourselves very vulnerable to another person. No one has to ponder too long to recognize the distortion that sexual abuse brings to this God–given act of marriage. The following list may be helpful in identifying some of the many and varied reactions brought about by sexual abuse. But somehow, with God's help, we, as victims, must regain our dignity and learn to share our dignity with our mates.

Characteristic Attitudes and Responses toward Sex of Female Sexual Abuse Victims

Need for male approval

Guilt and dirty feelings after sex or about sex

Problems concerning boundaries in sex

Inability to tolerate own body

Dissociation from own body

Feeling of worthlessness if unable to provide sex

Inability to look at a naked man/feeling of revulsion

Phobic avoidance of penises

Inability to tell whether or not men are "coming on"

Mixing of fear with sexual feelings

Effort to make "it" (life) better with sex

Avoidance of sexual activity or use of words associated with sex

Compulsive sexual behavior

Prostitution

Sexual acting out

Lack of sexual desire

Extreme modesty

Alternation between compulsive sexual behavior and lack of sex drive

Fear of letting go during sex/stopping self in
    arousal and enjoyment
Crying during or after sex
Need for darkness during sex
Difficulty with or inability to achieve orgasm
Need to feel helpless during sex
Fantasizing of rape
Aversion to masturbation
Pain in vaginal area during sex
Inability to have drug– or alcohol–free sex
Preoccupation with other concerns during sex
Eagerness for sex to be over
Feeling of having to perform during sex
Inability to ask to have sexual needs met
Anger during and after sex at having been
    exploited
Inability to be playful during sex
View of self as sex object

With God's help victims and victims'
spouses will learn how to overcome harmful
memories and reactions. Holding hands until
the victim feels safe or committing to only
holding one another for a time can be a good
beginning. Often it helps victims to know from
their partners that they would be loved by them
even if the couple never had sex.

Intimacy carries the overwhelming challenge of commitment. But there is no greater
expression of love than the deep intimacy of
knowing. Knowing another and being known
is to destroy the darkness. This is intimacy;
this is love.

DEFYING THE DARKNESS—
THE PERPETRATOR AND
THE CONFRONTATION

Victims are often overwhelmed with fear and helplessness at the thought of their perpetrator(s). But as they become aware of the truth about their perceived helplessness, they gain strength, and as their recovery gradually progresses, they find that fear has disappeared and been replaced by God's wisdom. This wisdom will help in understanding the recommended method of confrontation.

A common reaction to the subject of confrontation is anger. Simply reading the word *perpetrator* may have made some readers angry. If, as you are able to read through this chapter, you will make notes when you feel especially angry, they will help in your eventual confrontation. If your anger is consuming you, reread chapter 9, which deals with overcoming anger. Then, at a later time try again to read this present chapter.

Many perpetrators will not express sorrow for the sin nor choose to start recovery; some who start will not put forth the hard work necessary to complete the journey; and others, to avoid prosecution, will only pretend to start. Still others will say a recovery process is not necessary because the abuse never happened.

Characteristically, perpetrators are "me first" individuals who think of their own pleasure. Some have dominant personalities and may exercise tyrannical control of their homes. Often they are unable to have meaningful relationships with persons in their own age group, and they are usually emotionally dependent upon others and unable to express their emotional needs appropriately.

Just as with victims, perpetrators can be male or female, adolescents or adults, rich or poor. Perpetrators can be fathers, mothers, brothers, sisters, baby–sitters, uncles, aunts, neighbors, or strangers. Perpetrators can be doctors, pastors, lawyers, teachers, as well as vagrants. They can come from any place within the family and from any place within society.

Personality characteristics frequently found in perpetrators include poor impulse control, low self–esteem, self–pity; involvement in substance abuse; and the use of pornography, both for their own stimulation and for attracting possible victims. They may have been emotionally deprived in childhood, victims themselves, with a great deal of responsibility in their families of origin.

Perpetrators may come from family systems that did not set appropriate boundaries, characterized by chaotic home situations in which no family members had their needs appropriately met. Some perpetrators' families may have attempted to isolate their children from the community or overprotect them. Rigid and extreme religious and moralistic attitudes are common.

Offenders who have come from an abusive background are not justified by that fact, but knowledge of the details of the background helps counselors in guiding their recovery process. There is hope for the perpetrator, but the required long process of recovery absolutely cannot be taken lightly. The perpetrator's having said "I'm sorry" is simply not enough basis for believing that restoration has occurred. The abuser made a choice to abuse.

Confronting the abuser is a normal part of a recovery program for victims of sexual abuse. Confrontations may take place face to face with perpetrators, or in mock confrontations. Confrontations should include victims' expressions of how they feel about the effects of their abuse, and about their perpetrator.

Confrontation holds extraordinary importance in the family setting, where, for reconciliation to take place, the victim must, in most situations, directly confront the abuser. At the time of disclosure all family members, including members of the extended family, need to be informed of the identity of the perpetrator, for two reasons: 1) the victim must be protected, in the not uncommon case of the perpetrator's relapse; and 2) for the protection of all other potential victims in the family system.

Disclosure also allows every family member to be a support to the recovery process of both the victim and the perpetrator. There is absolutely no intent to shame the perpetrator or to provide information about the victim. It is extremely important to honor the victim's privacy concerning the abuse. However, it is also necessary to provide some facts about the perpetrator and the nature of the abuse if all opportunities for recovery are to be available to the victim and those involved in counseling.

A confrontation between victim and perpetrator together with a professional in a safe environment can also be a first step to the perpetrator's apology session. At a later time the perpetrator needs to meet with the entire family and ask forgiveness from each member. The victim and other siblings may find the process difficult, but it plays an important part in keeping the spouse and the siblings in an incestuous family from being second (and further) victims.

Victims must prepare themselves for possible rejection at the confrontation. Many abusers only abuse again. In many states, children as young as five must face their perpetrators in court. This often revictimizes the victim, so it is of utmost importance to be very careful and mindful of confrontation.

Mock confrontation is often used in therapy sessions where a safe environment is absolutely essential. The victim may confront an empty chair, a picture of the perpetrator, or any other association–producing object or setting that will allow the victim to confront the perpetrator as if he or she were actually present. This step has major importance in recovery as it enables victims to release the strong emotions stuffed inside them and begin to regain their lost power from the abuser. The presence of a professional in this kind of confrontation is clearly indicated.

If direct confrontation is to be a part of the recovery process, seek God's help as well as that of a professional counselor. If reconciliation is to be a part of your process, pray to God for the restoration of relationships. But remember, reconciliation will never include abuse, only peace and unity.

Confronting a perpetrator by playing a tape of the victim's message during their meeting is very effective. Victims are not forced to shut down if the perpetrator becomes verbally or emotionally abusive during the confrontation, and they are also able to include all that they wish to say to the perpetrator. Another advantage is that if the confrontation becomes too emotional, victims can take time for things to settle down by shutting off the tape.

Typical reactions of perpetrators to confrontation include remorse, denial, and false interpretation of the abuse event. Remorseful offenders are the most likely to accept responsibility for the abuse and to undergo genuine repentance. Offenders who refuse to acknowledge that anything happened may not be willing to admit to having committed a crime punishable by incarceration or may have an intense need to justify and protect themselves from recognizing and feeling the extent of their offense. Some of these perpetrators have sociopathic traits, have little guilt, and volubly deny any involvement. Without intensive treatment, they will continue to be a great danger to society, and will very likely victimize someone again. Some offenders who admit to the offending behavior and insist that it is not a crime argue that they are actually helping by teaching the child how to have sex, in fact improving the child's quality of life. These persons are pedophiles, offenders who deliberately set up situations in which children can be victimized. Confrontations with them are usually not effective, and it is more than likely that the victim will be revictimized in a confrontation.

Face–to–face confrontation of perpetrators of ritualistic sexual abuse is not always possible or even advised, for various reasons. Rather, mock confrontation should be used. The aggressor(s) may not be known to the victim, or the victim may have been drugged during the abuse or used in a ritual child–dedication ceremony now lost in the victim's memory. Perpetrators may be dangerous, and in any case, the Word of God specifically forbids having anything to do with such evil.

Criminally insane perpetrators and those who display the evil characteristics listed in Romans 1:29–32 should also be dealt with only in a setting of mock confrontation; great caution is required in face–to–face encounters with unstable minds.

When recovery has progressed to the right point for confrontation, the victim must make a conscious decision to face the perpetrator with the result of his or her crime. Decide whether what has been learned points toward a personal confrontation or a mock one, but use the encounter to release feelings of hurt and anger. It is essential to have the help of a professional as to when to confront and whether the confrontation should be done personally or symbolically. Be sure that the confrontation takes place in a safe environment and have other people present for potential support. If there is more than one abuser, each one should be confronted individually. The victim should not rationalize, apologize, or make excuses for them, but directly confront the aggressor with honest feelings concerning the effects of the abuse.

Many victims need to explore their own mixed feelings toward their perpetrator(s). In situations where the perpetrator is a family member or a highly valued person, such as a youth pastor or inspiring teacher, the presence of contradictory emotions and feelings is a common phenomenon and must be sorted through by the victim. For the victim of rape by a stranger, mixed feelings are not likely to be a problem, but none of them should be swept under the spiritual rug. As Christians, we may think we have taken care of all our feelings because we want the offender to be with Christ, and we may spend time praying for him/her. We must respect all the emotions God has given us and process any damaging ones we discover.

Mixed feelings are particularly frequent in child incest victims, who may have a very strong attachment to their perpetrators and want to protect them from any consequences of their abusive behavior. These victims do want the abuse to stop, but they do not want the relationship to stop. What they want and have always wanted is a healthy, caring relationship.

All victims must process their mixed feelings of love and hate if a healthy attitude toward the perpetrator is to be developed. Those feelings may be as unhealthy as hate that never leads to forgiveness or fear that submerges honest responses to putdowns and false assumptions. Victims, to become overcomers, must not only assign accountability to the perpetrator verbally and physically, but emotionally as well. We are no longer the caretakers of the perpetrator.

Don't feel shame or guilt about having enjoyed the healthy part of your relationship with family perpetrators. Childhood incest victims should have been able to share a healthy, loving relationship with their parents. And just as you may physically have enjoyed the stimulation received in sexual abuse through normal physiological reaction, you would also have enjoyed the healthy emotional stimulation. Sexual abuse not only touches the body, but it also touches the mind.

STAYING IN THE LIGHT—
FRIENDS AND HELPERS

This final chapter is addressed to the family, friends, and professional caregivers who form the sexual abuse survivor's support system, in the hope that you may be a light to your special one who is emerging from the darkness.

Learning of the abuse of a loved one is difficult for the family and the friends of a victim. To be able to give the support you want to your loved one, it is essential for you to find someone who will help you through your own pain, guilt, and anger. Giving the important gift of time for healing will place heavy demands on you, but it is impossible to describe how much difference there is between the progress of the victim who receives support and the one who does not. Loving support will almost always reduce the recovery time for the victim.

The importance of loving support from friends and other helpers can hardly be overemphasized. Many well–intentioned people, however, further injure the victim and hinder her healing process through shallow, quick–fix solutions. Such statements may result from lack of understanding of sexual abuse issues or the severity of the statements for the victim, exhaustion with the victim or the recovery process, or the desire to avoid dealing with this demanding, time–consuming, and possibly threatening situation.

"The Don'ts"

Don't say to the victim:
1. I don't believe you were ever abused.
2. Why can't you just forget it?
3. That's in the past. Why keep bringing it up?
4. Can't you just let go? It's not happening now.
5. Why are you making such a big deal? You were only three.
6. Just pray about it. Give it to God.
7. You are the problem, not what happened.
8. Why didn't you stop it?
9. Stop thinking about it. It's a sin. The Bible says to think on things that are good.
10. What did you do to cause it to happen?
11. Why can't you hurry up and get over this?
12. Paul said to forget the past and to move on toward the future.
13. You're not forgiving. You have to forgive or God won't help you.

14. I am so sick of this, what about me?
15. You have got to quit feeling sorry for yourself.

Whatever the reasons are for making statements like these, they must be recognized as statements that bring darkness, a kind of death, to the victim. They can also be very painful for the friends and families of victims due to the deep emotional scars inflicted by sexual abuse.

A real problem for friends is in being able to see the urgency of the need for support of a victim, especially through a lengthy healing process. Because the brokenness of a heart cannot be seen in the same way that the brokenness of a bone is evident (by x–ray if not by outward appearance), its presence is not so readily recognized.

At the early stage of the sexual abuse victim's recovery, friends may be called to give more than the victim, who is often simply not capable. For example, a wife who was in denial did not want to have sexual intercourse with her husband. He was angry and didn't want to pay for her counseling or participate in the therapy, which required abstinence from sex for a period of time. But, reconciling himself, he was able to reach deep inside to help his wife. And because he chose to show interest in her recovery and become part of the healing process, she came to experience and appreciate the miracle of intimacy that God intended for couples through sex. Through

God's blessing of their efforts to help each other, their story ended in victory.

Friends of victims can add further support by contributing these "Dos":

"The Dos"

Do stand ready...
1. To give support.
2. To give acceptance.
3. To give love.
4. To give time.
5. To give understanding.
6. To give interest.
7. To give forgiveness.
8. To give help.
9. To give belief.
10. To give prayer.
11. To give encouragement.
12. To give hope.
13. To give honor.
14. To give trust.
15. To give validation.

A further step of support is to be a receptive listener when your special survivor is called upon to read a letter he or she has been asked to write as part of the workbook assignments included in the recovery program. Your attention will be meaningful.

May God let you know His will and approve those things essential to the recovery, and may you as a friend, be able to "hang onto" godly wisdom in the support process.